Tears of a Tiger

by
Sharon M. Draper

Teacher Guide

Written by
Linda Sasser

Edited by
Katherine E. Martinez

Note

The Simon and Schuster paperback edition of this book, ©1994, was used to prepare this guide. The page references may differ in other editions.

Please note: This novel deals with sensitive, mature issues (e.g., death, suicide). Please assess the appropriateness of this book for the age level and maturity of your students prior to reading and discussing it in your class.

ISBN 1-58130-670-9

Printed in the United States of America.

To order, contact your local school supply store, or—

Novel Units, Inc.
P.O. Box 791610
San Antonio, TX 78279

Web site: www.educyberstor.com

Table of Contents

Summary 3

About the Author 3

Introductory Activities 3

Vocabulary Activities 4

Eleven Sections 8
Each section contains: Vocabulary, Discussion Questions, and Supplementary Activities

Post-reading Discussion Questions 24

Post-reading Extension Activities 24

Assessment 27

Skills and Strategies

Thinking
Research, critical thinking, compare/contrast, decision making

Comprehension
Analysis, predictions, sequencing, application

Writing
Letter writing, poetry, newspaper reporting

Vocabulary
Target words, synonyms, context clues

Listening/Speaking
Class discussion, guest speakers

Literary Elements
Characterization, imagery, allusion, narrative style

Fine Arts
Art, drama, music

Summary

Tears of a Tiger is the story of Andy Jackson, a teenager who accidentally kills his best friend, Robert Washington, after drinking and driving. Andy struggles with the pain and guilt of bearing the responsibility for the death of Rob. Turning away from his friends and family, Andy ends his own life believing it will end everyone's suffering.

Please note: This novel deals with teenage depression and suicide. Please assess the appropriateness of this novel for the students in your class.

The story is artfully told through English class assignments, including poetry; snippets of dialogue; journal entries and letters; and police and newspaper reports. Consequentially, both past and present tense are used in this Teacher Guide. Also, this guide is organized by page number due to the brief nature of each of the novel's chapters.

About the Author

Sharon M. Draper was the 1997 National Teacher of the Year and was honored at the White House by President Clinton. She won first prize in the 1991 *Ebony* Magazine literary contest for her short story, "One Small Touch." She currently resides in Cincinnati, Ohio, where she is the head of the English Department at Walnut Hills High School.

Introductory Activities

1. Previewing the Book: Have the students examine the title and read the synopsis on the back cover. Students can write their predictions about what will happen in the novel.

2. Narrative Style: The story is told from the points of view of the group of friends involved. Discuss as a class what might be good or bad about this style of narration.

3. Character Journal: List the names of the main characters from the story *Tears of a Tiger* and have each student choose one. As students read the novel, they write regular journal entries from that character's point of view. Journal entries relate to the events of the story. Students should be prepared to share their thoughts with their classmates.

4. Attribute Web: Have students create an attribute web (see p. 5 of this guide) for each of the following ideas: friendship, personal responsibility, guidance, faith. Focus on one word at a time. Write each word in the center of a large piece of paper and ask the students to quickly tell what each word brings to mind. Encourage students to elaborate on each other's ideas.

5. Story Map: Every story has the same elements—a setting, a problem, and events that lead up to the resolution or conclusion. Have the students complete the story map on p. 6 of this guide to help them summarize the novel.

6. Grid: Ask students if they have ever experienced peer pressure. Tell them to describe the situation and their solution to the problem. Was there a lesson learned from the experience? Complete the decision-making grid on p. 7.

7. Bulletin Board: On a bulletin board, display pictures or illustrations of tigers. Have students think about the title, *Tears of a Tiger*. Discuss some possible interpretations of the book's title.

Vocabulary Activities

1. Context Clues: Many words used in the novel are modified slang words. As the students read, have them create a list of some of the words used in the novel that reflect the language of the young people in the story. Define each of the words by using context clues.

2. Word Wall: Assign each student one or two vocabulary words from each section. The student looks up the correct meaning for each word in the dictionary and illustrates the word. The student will display the drawing in the classroom as well as define the word for classmates. Students are expected to keep a log of all words and their meanings in a vocabulary notebook.

3. Target Words: Assign each student one vocabulary word from each section. They are to create a poster, banner or sign to highlight their word. They must include the meaning of the word, how it is pronounced, and use it in a sentence. The products may be displayed in the classroom.

4. Synonym Match: Have students select vocabulary words from the section and list one synonym for each vocabulary word on a small piece of paper. Pairs or groups of students mix up the pieces of paper and match each synonym to the appropriate vocabulary word.

5. Vocabulary Charades: Place the vocabulary words in a basket. Have the students draw out a word and act it out to the class. This can be done individually, with a partner, or in small groups. You can also pick specific words from the novel that you wish to target.

6. Sentences: Have the students select five or six vocabulary words and use as many as possible in one sentence.

Attribute Web

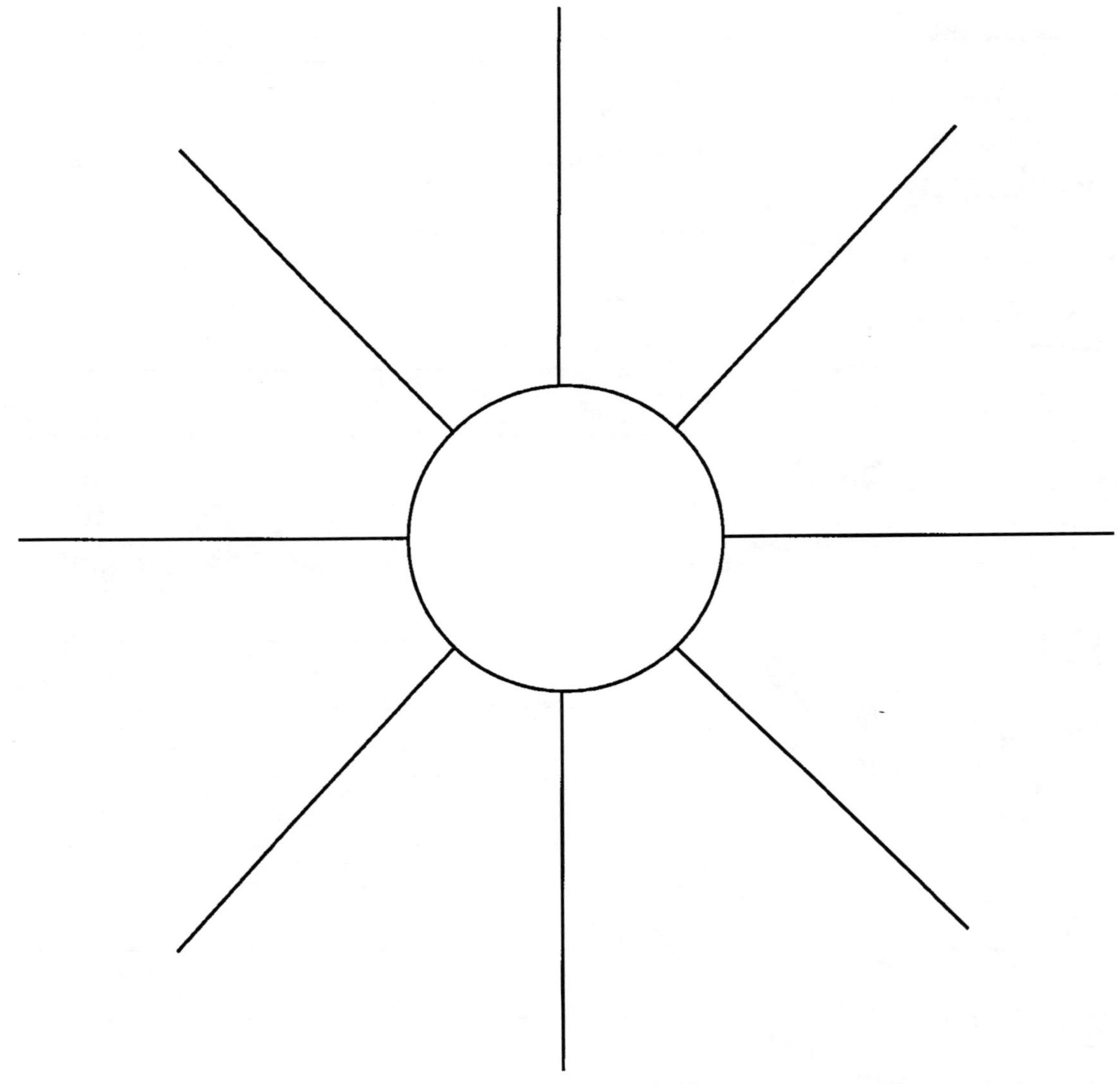

Story Map

Setting

Problem

Goal

Episodes

Resolution

Characters_______________________________________

____

Time and Place_______________________________________

____

Problem_______________________________________

____

____

Goal_______________________________________

____

____

Beginning ⟶ Development ⟶ Outcome

____

____

____

____

Resolution_______________________________________

____

____

____

Decision-Making Grid

The decision-making grid below is supposed to make it easier to find the best solution to a problem. Fill in the grid below by specifying a certain problem in your own or Andy's life. Then come up with four possible ways to solve the problem. After filling in the grid completely and choosing one solution, share your choice with your classmates and see if they agree with you.

Problem	Criterion #1:	Criterion #2:	Criterion #3:
State the problem:	Will the solution hurt someone?	Will it make me feel better?	
Solution #1:			
Solution #2:			
Solution #3:			
Solution #4:			

Pages 1-22

Vocabulary

fiery (1) | weaving (1) | retaining (1) | frantically (2)
opposing (3) | raggedy (4) | honorable (4) | cold-blooded (5)
dizzy (12) | dashboard (12) | stunted (16) | infinite (16)
outrageous (16)

Discussion Questions

1. What does the newspaper article report in the first chapter? *(Four boys went out after the basketball game. Robert Washington is killed in a car accident, and the three other passengers escape injury.)*
2. Who is Andy dating? *(Keisha)*
3. Why do the other boys tease Andy about Keisha? *(They tell Andy that Keisha "has him on a leash.")*
4. What are the four friends going to do after the game? *(drink beer and try to find a party)*
5. Who does not drink alcohol? *(B.J.)*
6. What kind of car does Andy drive? *(a red Chevette)*
7. Which member of the team decides to go home after the game instead of going with the guys? *(Gerald)*
8. Who calls Keisha to inform her about the accident? *(her friend, Rhonda)*
9. Why does Rhonda assume that it was Andy who was involved in the accident? *(The police reveal that a red Chevette was involved in an accident.)*
10. Who was the only person admitted into the hospital? *(Andy)*
11. Who had the most to drink, according to Tyrone? *(Andy)*
12. Why do you think the police questioned Tyrone first? *(Answers will vary.)*
13. How was Rob positioned in the car? *(His seat was pushed all the way back and his legs were on top of the dash.)*
14. Why did B.J. sit behind Rob? *(B.J. was the shortest and Rob needed to push his seat the farthest back because he was tall.)*
15. Who was the first to escape from the car? *(Tyrone)*
16. Why couldn't the boys save Rob from the explosion? *(The car door was bent shut, preventing them from pulling Rob out.)*

17. Who did Rob call to for help? Why? *(Andy; Answers will vary.)*

18. Why does B.J. look to God for answers? *(Answers will vary.)*

19. What excuse does B.J. give the guys for not drinking alcohol? *(He says it stunted his growth.)*

20. Why didn't B.J. drive when he was the only sober one in the car? *(He never thought about it. He was just happy to be part of the group.)*

21. Why does B.J. decide to go back to church? *(to help him deal with a problem that is bigger than he is)*

22. Which of the boys had the idea of getting the alcohol, according to Rhonda? *(Rob)*

23. What is ironic about Andy being appointed as the new team captain for the basketball team? *(Rob was the team captain before he died in the crash.)*

Supplementary Activities

1. Research: Have students research the number of deaths that are caused by drivers under the influence of alcohol between the ages of 15-20.

2. Critical Thinking: Students should discuss how they think this crash and the death of Rob will affect the lives of Andy, B.J., and Tyrone. What can the boys do to help them deal with the loss of their friend and the pain that they are feeling?

3. Critical Thinking: Have students look at the conversational way the characters speak. When might this story take place? Why do you think the author uses this style of narration? Is it significant that young people tell much of the story?

4. Listening/Speaking: Invite a local police officer to speak to the class about the dangerous effects of alcohol and to share statistics about drinking and driving.

5. Writing: Have the students pretend that they are a friend of Rob's. Write a eulogy for Rob.

Pages 23-34

Vocabulary

scholarship (24)	proceeded (25)	courage (25)	miscellaneous (26)
recuperated (26)	ordeal (26)	homicide (27)	revoked (27)
privileges (28)	forfeited (28)	adjusting (31)	hollers (32)
offends (33)	clogged (34)	eliminate (34)	

Discussion Questions

1. How does everyone treat Andy after the accident occurs? *(They try to understand his pain.)*

2. How is Andy dealing with the tragedy? Do you agree or disagree with his method of coping? *(Answers will vary.)*

3. Who was Rob the closest to out of the three boys? *(Tyrone)*

4. How had Andy become friends with Rob? *(They had gotten into a fight with one another and became friends afterward.)*

5. Who believes he is going to be the next Spud Webb? Why is B.J. so determined to play on the basketball team? *(B.J.; Answers will vary.)*

6. What could Andy have done to avoid the accident? *(He could have chosen not to drink and drive.)*

7. Why did Andy cry when he was in court? *(Answers will vary.)*

8. What sentence did the judge give to Andy? *(Andy has his license revoked until he turns 21, and a two-year suspended sentence.)*

9. Do you believe that the punishment Andy received fit the crime he committed? *(Answers will vary.)*

10. What does Andy have to do in order to be eligible to play basketball? *(not miss any Alcohol Rehabilitation classes and keep his grades up)*

11. How does Rhonda feel about the grief counselors who visit the school? Why do you think she feels this way? *(Answers will vary.)*

12. Who is Rhonda dating? *(Tyrone)*

13. Why does Gerald hate peanut butter? *(His mom always made peanut butter and jelly sandwiches; she left his family, but the peanut butter remained.)*

14. What are the things that Gerald says a five-dollar bill can buy? Why does Gerald mention these things? *(a bottle of whiskey, a nickel bag of pot, a rock of crack, and a six-pack of beer; Answers will vary, his stepfather uses these things.)*

Supplementary Activities

1. Critical Thinking: Separate students into small groups. Students should come to a consensus, just as a jury would, regarding the actions of Andy, B.J., and Tyrone. Each group should assign a spokesperson to report for the group. Discuss as a class.

2. Writing: Gerald writes an essay on three things he would eliminate if he could change the world. As a class, brainstorm a similar list of things the world could do without.

3. Critical thinking: Have the students reread both sections relating to Rhonda and Gerald's reactions to the car accident. Discuss as a class how and why the accounts differ. Which reaction is more thought-provoking? Why?

4. Research: Students are to research what sentence a 17-year-old student would receive if charged with a DWI and vehicular homicide in their state. Discuss why states do not have the same punishment for the same type of crime. How does Andy's punishment compare to their own state? Students can summarize their findings in writing.

Pages 35-49

Vocabulary

assuming (35) moody (35) capable (36) frenzied (37)
severe (38) psychic (39) undergraduate (41) dispense (42)
affected (42) initial (45) convert (46) cotillions (46)
affirmative action (47) rebellious (48)

Discussion Questions

1. Why is Andy late to the basketball game? *(He had to ride the bus since he can no longer use his car.)*
2. Who has replaced Rob as center on the basketball team? *(Andy)*
3. Do you feel that Andy should take the place of Rob as both team captain and as center? *(Answers will vary.)*
4. Why do you think Andy played better than ever for his first game back? *(Answers will vary.)*
5. What does Andy believe made the team want to win and not give up? *(seeing Rob's parents cheer for them in the stands)*
6. How does the author let you know that Andy is unhappy with his parents? *(the comments that he makes about his parents to friends and Dr. Carrothers)*
7. How would you describe Andy's coach as a person? Do you think he helps Andy? *(Answers will vary.)*
8. Why does Coach believe it is good for Andy to cry? *(It helps to cleanse the soul.)*
9. Who is Dr. Carrothers? *(Andy's psychologist)*
10. What impresses Andy about Dr. Carrothers? *(Dr. Carrothers makes over ninety dollars an hour.)*
11. Why does Andy feel that Rob wouldn't blame him for the accident? *(Rob was easygoing and nothing would ever bother him.)*
12. Why do you think Andy says he is not a killer? *(Answers will vary.)*
13. Why do you think Andy didn't want to role-play with Dr. Carrothers? *(Answers will vary.)*
14. Why did Dr. Carrothers conduct an initial interview with Andy's parents before talking to Andy? *(to get to know Andy and what his interests are)*
15. How does Andy describe his mom to Dr. Carrothers? *(She has no grip on reality, she is very active in her sorority functions, and the two are nothing alike.)*
16. What is Andy's attitude toward his father? *(He seems resentful and disgusted with his father.)*

17. How does Andy feel about his brother, Monty? *(Andy says that Monty is the only one in his family who is "really cool.")*

18. Why is Andy concerned about Monty? *(Monty is interested in blond girls and thinks that being black is not cool.)*

19. Why does Andy feel both guilty and proud about taking Rob's position in basketball? *(Answers will vary.)*

Supplementary Activities

1. Drama: Pair off students and have them role-play, pretending to be either Rob or Andy. What would Andy say if Rob were talking to him about the accident? What would Rob tell Andy to do with his life and to help deal with his death?

2. Writing: Students can pretend to be Dr. Carrothers. What notes would they write down after their initial meeting with Andy? What impressions would Dr. Carrothers have about Andy's relationship with his family?

Pages 50-70

Vocabulary

adventure (51)	righteous (51)	tantrums (51)	engraved (53)
expectations (55)	radiator (55)	auditorium (56)	fortunate (57)
potential (57)	assumes (58)	frustration (59)	enhanced (59)
shimmers (66)	grace (68)	dense (69)	

Discussion Questions

1. Why do you think Andy is finally in a good mood? *(Answers will vary.)*

2. How is Andy reacting to Keisha not spending enough time with him? *(He begins to resent that she won't make more time for him.)*

3. What is happening to Andy's grades? *(His grades are slipping because he is not completing work.)*

4. Why do you think that Andy lets his grades slip? *(Answers will vary.)*

5. Why is Andy feeling more pressure from his parents about his grades? *(College is getting closer for him.)*

6. How did Gerald get the scar that is on his face? *(His dad beat him up and knocked him against the radiator.)*

7. How did Marcus acquire his nickname "curve buster"? *(He always passes his tests with A's.)*

8. What excuse does Andy give for not making straight A's? *(He doesn't want to be called to the front for recognition with all of the white kids and be laughed at by his friends.)*

9. According to Andy, how does his dad communicate with him? *(Andy's dad lectures, preaches, or yells.)*
10. Why doesn't Andy talk to the guidance counselor at school? *(Her breath smells and she once talked him out of a career he was interested in.)*
11. What does Dr. Carrothers mean when he states, "It's like the system is set up so you don't succeed"? *(Answers will vary.)*
12. Why do you think Keisha is frustrated with Andy? *(Answers will vary.)*
13. Describe the poem that Andy wrote. How does it make you feel? How do you think Andy felt when he wrote it? *(Answers will vary.)*
14. Why does the teacher compare poetry to rap music? *(so that the students can relate to how poetry is formed and what it expresses)*
15. Why do you think Andy doesn't turn in the poem he wrote? *(Answers will vary.)*

Supplementary Activities

1. Poetry Analysis: As a class, discuss each poem that the characters in *Tears of a Tiger* write. After completing the chart for each poem, compare and contrast them.

Author of Poem	Subject of Poem	Tone/Mood Poem Expresses	Style/Form of Poetry

2. Critical Thinking: Andy completes his poetry assignment, but after the teacher discusses what poetry is about, he decides not to turn it in. Gerald, on the other hand, has not done the assignment but after hearing the teacher's discussion of poetry, he opts to do it. Have the students discuss the teacher's influence on the two boys. What did the teacher say that changed Andy's mind? Why did Gerald decide to complete the assignment after all? What influence does a teacher have on a class? How do the students feel about writing poetry?

3. Writing: Andy discussed with Dr. Carrothers his views on discrimination. Have students write a one- to two-paragraph response to Andy's thoughts and feelings. Does racism still exist? What suggestions do they have about ending discrimination of any kind?

Pages 71-88

Vocabulary

cosmetic (71)	browsing (72)	commodities (72)	exaggerate (73)
vital (73)	looted (73)	phony (74)	cynical (74)
secure (77)	aspects (78)	donate (80)	concludes (80)
glistening (82)	cinder (84)	metaphor (85)	stereotypes (86)

Discussion Questions

1. Why is Christmas so tough for Andy to deal with? *(Rob and Andy used to spend Christmas together; it was a special time for the two friends.)*

2. Why did Andy feel like he and Rob were being watched at the store? *(He and Rob were both black and he felt that black people were always thought to be robbers and thugs by white people.)*

3. How does Andy feel about his relationship with Keisha? *(secure, happy)*

4. What spoils Christmas Day for Andy? *(Rob's mother calls, crying, to wish him a "Merry Christmas.")*

5. Why is Andy cynical about Christmas? *(He believes that people only want your money and that it is all phony.)*

6. Why do you think Andy would like school to be cancelled because of snow? *(Answers will vary.)*

7. How does Andy feel about his teacher, Ms. Blackwell? *(He calls her a "fire-breathin' dragon" and says her poetry is going to drive him crazy.)*

8. How does Gerald react to the poem, "One Thousand Nine Hundred and Sixty-Eight Winters"? *(He relates to it because when he tries to mind his own business, white people still are all around him. It's like he can't escape them, just as the speaker in the poem can't escape the white snow.)*

9. What does the snow in the poem refer to? *(black vs. white)*

10. What is the teacher's reasoning for using references of black and white in poetry? *(The tones of black and white have the greatest contrast so writers and poets use them as metaphors of contrast.)*

11. What did the color red represent in Puritan England over 300 years ago? Does the color represent anything today? *(evil, the devil; Answers will vary.)*

12. Why would Andy wonder if Rob's feet were cold like his own? *(Answers will vary.)*

Supplementary Activities

1. Research: Andy talks to Dr. Carrothers about racial issues and discrimination. The students should research laws that have been passed in the United States to help fight racism.

2. Literary Terms/Writing: Define what a metaphor is and identify metaphors used on page 85. Have the students pair off and write down as many original metaphors as they can think of. Share some of the metaphors.

3. Poetry: Have each student find a poem that uses color to create images in the mind. Have the students share their poems with the class.

Pages 89-105

Vocabulary

reality (89)	hypnotized (90)	verbalize (92)	traumatic (92)
grieving (93)	eliminate (93)	alternatives (93)	patient (98)
visions (99)	foolishness (99)	eternity (101)	treasure (105)

Discussion Questions

1. How does the winter weather reflect Andy's emotional state? *(Answers will vary; Andy feels cold and depressed, just as winter can be cold and depressing.)*

2. Why is Andy afraid to call Rob's parents? *(He doesn't have the nerve and he thinks that they hate him.)*

3. In what ways is Andy out of touch with reality? *(some ways he is out of touch include moodiness, crying, loss of ambition, nightmares, etc.)*

4. Why would the retaining wall seem bigger than it really is on the night of the accident? *(Answers will vary.)*

5. How does Andy describe his sadness and depression? *(He says that it's heavy, like carrying around Mike Tyson's punching bag inside.)*

6. How does Dr. Carrothers respond when Andy says, "It seems like bein' dead is the only way I'll ever feel alive again"? *(The doctor says that Andy wants to escape his pain, but that life is the answer.)*

7. What does Dr. Carrothers suggest Andy do in place of contemplating suicide? *(call Rob's parents or write Rob a letter)*
8. What does Andy tell Keisha he sees in his future? What event does this foreshadow? *(He sees nothing but darkness; Andy's suicide.)*
9. Why does Monty sleep with the light on? *(He is afraid of monsters.)*
10. Why would Andy feel that it would be a nightmare to be in a rich white neighborhood after midnight? *(Answers will vary.)*
11. Why would Monty be curious about the color of dreams? *(Answers will vary.)*
12. Why does Andy dream of Rob blaming Andy for his death? *(Andy feels guilty for what happened to his friend.)*
13. Do you think that Andy sent his letter to Rob's parents? *(Answers will vary.)*
14. What does Rob's family have that Andy believes his family doesn't have? *(closeness and love)*

Supplementary Activities

1. Compare/Contrast: Using the Venn diagram, compare and contrast the differences between Rob's family and Andy's family. The students should be prepared to share their ideas with classmates.

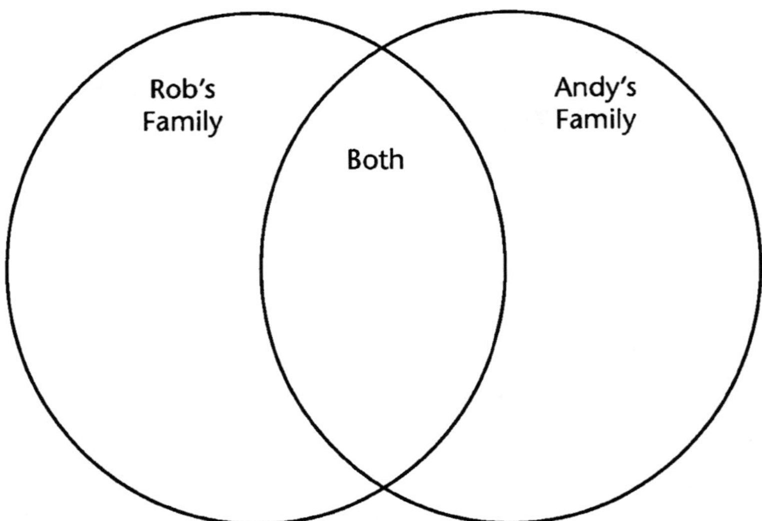

2. Critical Analysis: As a class, discuss Andy's dream about Rob. Do you believe Rob would want Andy to die? Why? Why is Andy having such nightmares?
3. Prediction: What do you think is going to happen to Andy as his emotional state continues to crumble?

Pages 106-122

Vocabulary

noble (106)	wretched (106)	morality (106)	degeneration (106)
inevitable (106)	deterioration (107)	coward (107)	strut (108)
confidences (112)	progressed (115)	uptight (118)	potential (120)
inhibitions (120)	intentions (122)		

Discussion Questions

1. Why does Ms. Blackwell think that Macbeth's death was inevitable? *(He was already dead inside.)*

2. How does Macbeth's emotional state compare to Andy's emotional state? *(They both feel dead inside, they have guilt on their conscience as they both killed their best friends, and they have both had to deal with devastating changes.)*

3. Why did Andy run out of his English class? *(Answers will vary; the discussion about Macbeth was too intense and similar to Andy's own ordeal.)*

4. What does B.J. always eat for lunch? Why? *(a baloney with mustard sandwich; because his mother takes the time to make him a nutritious lunch)*

5. Why does Andy get so upset when B.J. and Tyrone bring up Rob's name at lunch? *(Andy says he is trying to forget Rob but they won't let him when they reminisce about old times.)*

6. What hints do Tyrone and B.J. receive from Andy that tells them he is not able to handle the pain and pressure? *(Andy is moody and cries all the time. He acts very depressed unless Keisha is around.)*

7. What happens when Andy's friends try to talk to the counselor about Andy? *(She doesn't take them seriously and brushes them off.)*

8. Why would Andy hide the truth about his dreams, his failing grades, and his depression from Dr. Carrothers? *(Answers will vary.)*

9. Do you feel that Dr. Carrothers was right to end Andy's weekly visits so quickly? Why or why not? *(Answers will vary.)*

10. Why does Keisha believe that friends can survive anything? *(Her close friends are very kind and considerate and are her strength when she is dealing with major issues.)*

11. Why does Ms. Blackwell call Andy's parents? *(She is concerned about Andy and sees how he has changed in both his schoolwork and his attitude.)*

12. How does Andy's father react to Ms. Blackwell's call? *(He believes that she is overreacting to the situation and that Andy's behavior is normal for a teenager.)*

Supplementary Activities

1. Research: Have the students research what help is available to teenagers who are battling depression. Have them examine the ways that hotlines, centers, and school counseling address this issue. Make sure students are prepared to discuss their results with classmates.
2. Writing: Keisha writes a paper on the importance of friendship. Have the students write a paper that explains what friendship means to them.
3. Critical Thinking: Have students reread the Macbeth passage on page 108. How does this relate to Andy? What might Andy be thinking after hearing this passage read aloud? after hearing B.J.'s comments?

Pages 123-135

Vocabulary

dismissed (126)	stable (127)	hilarious (127)	ease (129)
extraordinary (131)	overwhelming (131)	magnificent (132)	electrify (132)
bombard (132)	daggers (134)		

Discussion Questions

1. How does Monty color people in his coloring book? *(He colors them with blond hair.)*
2. Why is Andy upset that Monty only likes blond-haired girls? *(Answers will vary.)*
3. Why did Monty put tears on his picture of a tiger? *(to make the tiger sad like Andy)*
4. Why doesn't Monty know the real reason as to why Andy can't drive? *(Answers will vary; Monty is only six years old so his parents have probably have not informed him of the details of his brother's accident.)*
5. Why would Monty compare Andy to a tiger? *(Answers will vary.)*
6. What does the teacher on page 126 of the text mean when she says that basketball might be Andy's escape? *(It is a way to vent his frustrations and take his mind off losing Rob.)*
7. Why does the teacher think that black kids are tougher than white kids? *(They need street smarts in order to survive.)*
8. What types of comments do the teachers make? *(judgemental comments: rap music is meaningless, mindless noise; black kids are tough, etc.)*
9. How have Keisha's feelings changed about dating Andy? *(She is tired of his crying and feels that he is getting too depressed, and she wants to ease up on their relationship.)*
10. What does Keisha notice about Andy when he is hosting the talent show? *(He is not smiling at all.)*

11. Why does Andy snap at Keisha during the talent show? *(Answers will vary.)*

12. Why does Keisha feel that it is time to break up with Andy? *(He is treating her badly and it is easier to break it off when you are fighting.)*

Supplementary Activities

1. Critical Thinking: Discuss as a class the conversation between the two teachers. What does this conversation tell you about the teachers' attitudes? How does their attitude relate to Andy and Gerald's feelings of discrimination?

2. Critical Thinking: Have students separate into small groups and compare Andy and Keisha's views on their relationship. How do Andy's feelings differ from Keisha's? Why? What do you think is going to happen to their relationship?

3. Compare/Contrast: Using the Venn diagram, have the students compare and contrast Keisha and Andy's relationship with Rhonda and Tyrone's relationship. Have the students write down the page numbers in which they have found examples to support their ideas.

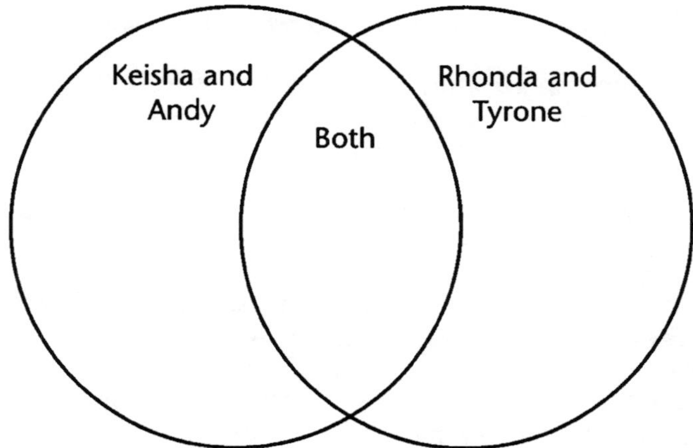

Pages 136-154

Vocabulary

unfortunate (137)	vaguely (138)	crept (139)	revelation (139)
resilient (139)	emerged (140)	dedicate (142)	bout (143)
hectic (148)	reprehensible (149)	punitive (149)	ambitions (150)
detriment (150)	dignified (150)	assimilate (153)	

Discussion Questions

1. Why didn't Andy's mom come to see him host the talent show? *(She claimed she had a sinus headache.)*

2. Why does Andy feel that he doesn't deserve to have someone as good as Keisha in his life? *(Answers will vary.)*

3. When talking to his mom, what incident from his childhood does Andy compare his pain to? *(He recalls being nine years old and almost drowning on vacation in South Carolina. He feels like he is choking and not able to breathe or call for help.)*

4. Why would Andy's cries for help only make him feel worse? *(The harder he tries to reach out to someone, the worse the pain becomes.)*

5. Why won't Andy's mother do more to console Andy? *(She is scared and unable to deal with the pain herself.)*

6. Why did Keisha decide not to sing the song that she was going to dedicate to Andy? *(Answers will vary; she was doing something special for Andy to make him feel better about himself, but he was cruel to her.)*

7. In her letter, Rhonda writes that Andy was no fun after Keisha stormed out of the talent show. Why did he change his attitude? *(He and Keisha had broken up, and he was feeling angry and guilty about how he had treated her.)*

8. What is the bad news Coach Ripley has for Andy? *(College basketball scouts were looking for Andy but couldn't locate him because Andy missed school that day.)*

9. What do you think is happening to Andy as he continues to hide his emotional problems and his fears from everyone? *(Answers will vary; Andy is slowly giving up on life and turning away from everyone who cares about him.)*

10. Why does Andy evade the conversation with his father? *(He is scared and doesn't want his father to know about his failing grades and his problems.)*

11. Why does Andy's father finally take Andy's problems seriously? *(He received Andy's report card in the mail and sees his failures; he is worried about his son.)*

12. Why is Andy defensive and angry toward his father? *(His father has never shown any concern before and Andy feels that it is too late now.)*

13. What reason does Andy's father give for calling him "Andrew"? *(He wanted his son to have a name he would be proud of and not use a nickname.)*

14. What must Andy do to make it in the world, according to Andy's father? *("Assimilate into the society in which we live" (p. 153); be accepted by white people.)*

15. Do you feel Andy's father did the right thing by approaching Andy in the manner that he did? Why or why not? *(Answers will vary.)*

Supplementary Activities

1. Critical Thinking: Discuss as a class how Andy is feeling about himself and his future. How does his father make him feel? What could his father have done to restore Andy's confidence? How would the students have approached Andy if they were a parent in this situation?

2. Critical Thinking/Writing: Andy's father talks extensively about having a son to be proud of. Have the students think about Andy and his relationship with his father. Each student should make a list using a T-chart of the positive and negative aspects of Andy and his father's relationship. Write a paragraph explaining what could be improved and how. They should use evidence from the text to support their claims.

Andy/Father Relationship

Positive	Negative

Pages 155-165

Vocabulary

adviser (156) soul (157) fatal (160) instinct (163)
ancestors (163) tufts (164)

Discussion Questions

1. Why does Andy suddenly feel the need to talk to someone? *(Answers will vary; He feels overwhelmed by guilt, unable to escape his pain.)*

2. Why won't Andy talk to Dr. Carrothers' associate, Dr. Kelly? *(It took Andy a long time to open up to Dr. Carrothers and he refuses to discuss his personal life with a stranger.)*

3. Why does Andy hate to talk to answering machines? *(He feels that they leave you naked and unprotected. It's like you left a little piece of yourself behind, exposed for others to examine.)*

4. Why is Andy more vulnerable than ever? *(He feels that there is no one for him to talk to.)*

5. How does Keisha feel about her breakup with Andy? *(She thinks it is for the best.)*

6. Where is Rhonda going after school? *(She is heading over to Andy's house to give him his missed work.)*

7. How is a caged tiger similar to Andy at this time? *(A caged tiger cannot go anywhere. Andy feels trapped, vulnerable, and unhappy.)*

8. Why is Andy feeling so cold and empty? *(He says that he can't stand the pain of living and wants the hurt to go away.)*

9. What other time in the story has Andy felt trapped this way? *(in a department store when his shoelace was caught in the escalator)*

Supplementary Activities

1. Prediction: What do you think Andy is going to do? Why?
2. Critical Thinking: The title *Tears of a Tiger* refers to Andy's character. How do the two relate? Why would the author choose a tiger and not another animal to depict Andy?

Pages 166-180

Vocabulary

disposition (166)	summoned (167)	bitter (168)	severity (169)
triumphed (169)	envied (174)	shattered (175)	irritable (178)

Discussion Questions

1. Who was the first to notice that something was wrong at Andy's house? *(Monty noticed blood.)*
2. Why does the suicide/grief counseling team visit the school? *(to help ease the students' pain over Andy's suicide and to get the students to discuss their thoughts and emotions)*
3. How does Tyrone feel about the suicide prevention team? *(He is bitter and angry and feels that they are too late.)*
4. Why do B.J. and Tyrone feel that the counselors cannot help them deal with the situation? *(Two of their friends have already died. B.J. and Tyrone tried to help Andy by going to the school counselor, but she wouldn't listen.)*
5. What advice does the team give the students to help them sort out their feelings and pain? *(write a letter to Andy)*
6. Does Tyrone understand Andy's suicide? *(No, because it was intentional. Rob's death was not intentional, it was an accident.)*
7. Who believes Andy is a coward for his actions? *(Gerald)*
8. Why is Gerald angry at Andy? *(Andy is making his friends face the death of another friend.)*
9. What has Marcus learned from this experience? *(to like himself, even though he has never been popular)*
10. What will Rhonda never be able to forget? *(finding Andy in his room, the blood, the screams, the tears, the funeral, and the pain)*
11. What does Keisha mean when she states, "You [Andy] had so much to live for"? *(Answers will vary; she is referring to his youth and his potential.)*

12. Why does Keisha write, "Wait for me" in her letter to Andy? *(Answers will vary.)*

13. What does B.J. say has kept him sane all of this time? *(the power and hope that comes from the Lord's forgiveness)*

14. What is B.J.'s tone in his prayer about Andy? *(B.J. is kind, gentle, and understanding.)*

15. What does Monty talk about when he visits Andy's grave? *(how his life has changed, missing Andy, being tough like a tiger, etc.)*

16. What has changed in Andy's family now that he is gone? *(His parents are separated and pay more attention to Monty.)*

17. What is one thing Monty says he will miss about Andy? *(having his big brother to teach him things in life, like how to play basketball and figure out girls)*

Supplementary Activities

1. Critical Thinking: The suicide/grief counseling team suggests that the students write a letter to Andy. What did the letter-writing accomplish? What other things might the counselors have done?

2. Writing: Have the students pretend that they are students at Hazelwood High School. Have them write a letter to Andy just as the students did. *(These might be too personal to share aloud.)*

3. Research: Have the students investigate groups such as S.A.D.D., MADD and other organizations against drinking and driving. Find out how each group originated and what they do to promote awareness and discourage drinking and driving.

Post-reading Discussion Questions

1. What is the effect of the author's narrative style?
2. What factors led to Andy's suicide?
3. If you had been one of Andy's friends, how would you have tried to help Andy deal with the pain and guilt?
4. What do you think will happen to Monty?
5. Foreshadowing is a literary technique used to give clues about future events in the story. What foreshadowing does the author use in *Tears of a Tiger?*
6. How might the story have been different if Rob had not died in the car accident? Would Andy and the other two boys feel any less guilty for drinking and driving? What would Andy's outlook have been if Rob survived?
7. How could Andy's family have intervened? Do they accurately perceive the depth of his depression? Why or why not?
8. What questions does this novel raise for you regarding teenage drinking? dealing with depression?
9. There were several discussions throughout the novel about racism. Why do you think the author included these discussions in the text?
10. What message was the author sending when writing this novel? How did she try to get her message across to the reader? Was she effective? Why or why not?

Post-reading Extension Activities

1. Write a new ending to the novel and read it to a classmate.
2. If you could meet the author, what questions would you ask her?
3. There are many events in the story that led to Andy's emotional decline. Plot the major events that occur throughout the story on the story map (p. 6 of this guide).
4. One of the issues that Andy deals with is racism. Do you feel that racism still exists today? Why? What are some possible solutions?
5. Using the attribute web on p. 5, place a character's name in the circle and descriptive words on the spokes. Use this to write a character sketch.
6. Create a mobile that depicts one of the character's personalities.

7. How do the characters in *Tears of a Tiger* change as the story progresses? Choose one character from the novel and complete a character chart (p. 26 of this guide) that shows how the character reacts to events in the story and how those events change the character.

8. When Andy is faced with problems in the story, he tries to solve them in different ways. Using the decision-making grid (p. 7 of this guide), try to evaluate different approaches Andy could have taken to solve his problems.

9. Choose one passage in the novel to read aloud. Find music that depicts the mood or feeling of that passage. Record the section of the story on tape along with the background music. Share your tape with the class.

Character Chart—Feelings

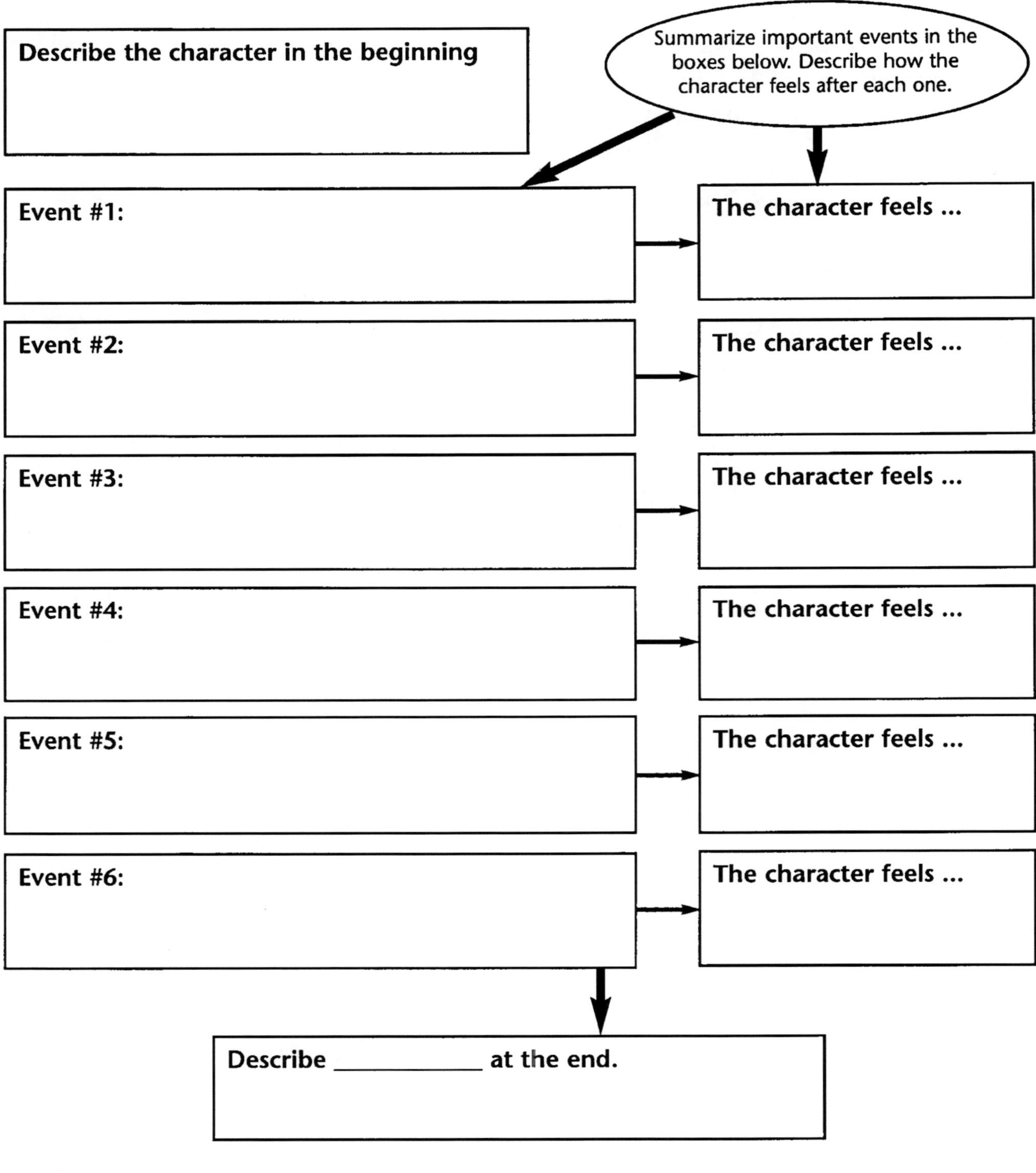

Assessment for *Tears of a Tiger*

Assessment is an ongoing process. The following ten items can be completed during the novel study. Once finished, the student and teacher will check the work. Points may be added to indicate the level of understanding.

Name ______________________________ Date ______________

Student	Teacher	
_____	_____	1. Using the descriptions from the novel, draw a picture of one of the characters.
_____	_____	2. Write a letter to Andy expressing your feelings about the events in the story.
_____	_____	3. Create a scrapbook that Monty would want to keep as a memory of Andy.
_____	_____	4. Imagine one of the characters ten years from now. Write a paragraph about what you think his/her life will be like and how s/he will remember Andy.
_____	_____	5. Write a poem that Monty might have written to Andy before or after Andy's death expressing his feelings.
_____	_____	6. Develop an attribute web (p. 5 of this guide) for the following characters: Andy, B.J., Keisha, Tyrone, and Gerald.
_____	_____	7. Research the laws your state has for driving under the influence. What is the punishment for breaking the law?
_____	_____	8. Create a collage that expresses the emotions you felt when you read the book.
_____	_____	9. Make a chart that shows the events that led to Andy's death.
_____	_____	10. Write about how one can help a friend who seems depressed.

Notes